BARBIE CHANG

# BARBIE CHANG

Victoria Chang

Copper Canyon Press
Port Townsend, Washington

Book cover: Phil Kovacevich

Copper Canyon Press is in residence at Fort Worden State Park in Port Townsend, Washington, under the auspices of Centrum. Centrum is a gathering place for artists and creative thinkers from around the world, students of all ages and backgrounds, and audiences seeking extraordinary cultural enrichment.

LIBRARY OF CONGRESS CATALOGING-IN-PUBLICATION DATA

Names: Chang, Victoria, 1970– author.
Title: Barbie Chang / Victoria Chang.
Description: Port Townsend, Washington : Copper Canyon Press, [2017]
Identifiers: LCCN 2017023244 | ISBN 9781556595165 (paperback : alk. paper)
Subjects: | BISAC: POETRY / American / Asian American.
Classification: LCC PS3603.H3575 A6 2017 | DDC 811/.6—dc23
LC record available at https://lccn.loc.gov/2017023244

9 8 7 6 5 4 3 2 FIRST PRINTING

Copper Canyon Press
Post Office Box 271
Port Townsend, Washington 98368

www.coppercanyonpress.org

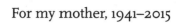

For my mother, 1941–2015

The soul is ambitious
for what is invisible.

JACK GILBERT, *REFUSING HEAVEN*

# CONTENTS

IV

BARBIE CHANG

## ONCE BARBIE CHANG WORKED

Once Barbie Chang worked on a
    street named Wall

once she sprinkled her yard with
    timed water once

she wore lanyards in large rooms
    all the chairs

pointed in the direction of one
    speaker and a podium

once she stood up at the end to
    leave but everyone

else stood up and began putting
    their hands together

and that started her always wanting
    something better

I

Barbie Chang parks next to the
    Soroptimist Park

to part her heart a hippopotamus
    of a heart a potomac

hurt why unearth her high school her
    children unearth

everything with their fingers and
    plastic shovels

chicken fingers and triangles of
    pizza everywhere

the beautiful thin mothers at school
    form a perfect circle

the Circle will school her if she lets
    them they have

something to say doves come out of
    their mouths that

explode into splinters in the sky
    Barbie Chang knows

that an outline of a tree can never be
    a tree that the opposite

of her fate is to not be born when she
    says she wants to be

visible she means she wants to be
      invisible she fell in

love with the Circle but she is allergic
      to them unnoticed by

them a streak of blue light in a blue
      sky she Skypes the

women at school each day only to learn
      that she is the last

person on earth the last leaf on the
      last tree there are

hints of fingerprints on the window
      but no more fingers

## BARBIE CHANG'S FATHER PAID

Barbie Chang's father paid her tuition
        by intuition his brain

now shuns all logic the law is thin with
        rules about love but

if a person is so edited that they are
        unrecognizable can you

still love them is it possible to write an
        elegy for someone who

isn't dead yet what if a name no longer
        means what it used

to where does the wind go when it
        is not blowing

today Barbie Chang packs up his
        clothes again to move him

to a facility to mute him no longer
        able to travel to Italy or

the local deli he tells Barbie Chang she
        is demented his dementia

is self centered it has no more center
        his words have lost

what they are trying to signify she drives
        away from his house for

the last time it's cold outside he stands
    at the front door waving

saying that he's fine that he's put on
    his *long distance shirt*

## BARBIE CHANG RUNS

Barbie Chang runs on a treadmill
    pinches her nose to see

what her mother's breathing feels like
    there's a name for it

*pulmonary fibrosis* but it is simply
    called suffocating

simply called dying die will die the
    trouble with being a

mother is that you too must die no
    more dice to roll the

last roll was the outcome all board
    games must come to

some end because of too much
    losing there is always

someone else doing something else
    everyone always cares

about someone else other people
    caring about something

else is called protesting on the news
    protesters come out again

police officers rotating in a line like
    a pinwheel there are always

new people dying a man alone on
    Everest under twenty

feet of snow who doesn't know much
    doesn't care about

the protesters there's always a woman
    worrying about other

women wanting to be loved by other
    women when Barbie

Chang was younger she thought the
    quiets before the storms

would last now she knows the storms
    will come in any form at

any time in the quiets she worries
    about the Circle in the

storms she thinks nothing about them
    and their fables it is

April again the storms have come again
    the man under the snow

digs a small circle around his mouth
    and takes his last breath

## ONCE BARBIE CHANG LOVED

Once Barbie Chang loved Mr. Darcy
    who had many

rivals who arrived at her doorstep each
    morning he had so

little body fat he never floated to the
    surface of the pool

Barbie Chang watched him disappear
    like a servant maybe

that's why she is always thirsty always
    looking for someone

else to make her worthy Barthes says
    lovers are wedged between two

*tenses of the now and the then* it's too early
    to say the mothers at

school have ruled her out they are the
    future tense the *then*

the Circle they form each day works
    as a ring around a

planet magnetic and genetic if she sticks
    her head out the window

as if she is on a train maybe night
    will take her head off

## BARBIE CHANG SHAKES

Barbie Chang shakes the hand of
    another Smith a former

beauty queen who still wins friends
    at school sets the

rules for who is cool and who is not
    Aristotle says that

desire is a reaching out for the sweet maybe
    Barbie Chang reaches

her hand into the center to not
    possess but to be

possessed the Smith appears sweet
    has nice teeth she is

taken aback that a Chang would be
    so strange and arrange

her own handshake without being
    asked first they both

gave birth but the Smith would never
    again say hello to that

Chang even one named Barbie unless
    she was the one performing

her children's surgery no matter how
    likely the Chang was to

change her time zones instantly clone
    herself to find a new

home she didn't yet know that certain
    suburban homes were filled

with people who wanted to be alone to
    dial certain phones

Barbie Chang's phone rings again the
    doctors are calling again

pretending that they are caring again no
    one but Barbie Chang

knows her father might have a tumor
    on his thyroid

he used to put on a tie to get promoted
    right around the carotid

he still knows his name is Fu but can no
    longer tie his own shoes

Barbie Chang can't stop watching
 the Ellen Pao trial

while the rest of the world wonders
 about a plane crash in

the Alps helping Ellen Pao is not an
 option Barbie Chang

opted out but never really severed
 ties with the people in

the office she kept quiet because by
 speaking she would

become a victim something projected
 upon like the canvas

that paint is thrown on she quietly
 packed her bag and

pulled it through the narrow door some
 say what a whore Ellen

Pao was to fall in love with a man in the
 office doesn't she know

that men like to take off their clothes
 extend their tongues

to see whose body it will run on some
 thought Ellen Pao was a

cyst in the office made lists in the office
    of all the wrong things

someone made a poll about her did she
    or didn't she was she or

wasn't she always the same binary argument
    racism or incompetence is

there a third possibility that when we
    have seen something so

many times we no longer recognize it as
    injustice our heads

are always only one foot away from
    the man's head in

the other hotel room but we don't notice
    because we can't see him

around an empty office building dead
    birds lie in the grass new

ones each day hit the glass each face
    the same expression

forever frozen in its own form like
    a stamp

## MR. DARCY LEANS

Mr. Darcy leans into Barbie Chang again
    weans her from his lean

then leans again his face doesn't reach
    her face but she can feel

its heat soldering her to him his shoulder
    lacks flesh but she still

wishes for it when he says *cheese* she
    shows her teeth and

wonders when she will believe in the
    idea of white space again

when she hangs a child's picture of
    a bird on the wall

some of the glitter falls off each day
    why does love feel

like a slow drip without a puddle a faded
    paddle on the beach

that the eye cannot see fading an open
    door and the triangle of

light trying to separate sometimes
    children hold hands

and spin until one gets so dizzy she
    spins out and away from

the group it's impossible to outline
    a beating heart

## IS A WINDCATCHER

Is a windcatcher still a windcatcher
    if there is no wind

moving it is Barbie Chang still a
    woman if there is no

man hunting her if she does not
    look in the mirror

does she exist if she walks past men
    and they do not look

at her is she still alive is a signified
    without a signifier

really impossible can that which is
    signified ever become

a signifier what is a birdfeeder
    without a bird is a

woman the birdfeeder the bird or
    the birdseed the moon

at night stretches on her bed like a
    blue dress when it

goes down a child foolishly believes
    it is gone

## THE PROGNOSIS IS POOR

The prognosis is poor again the lungs
    are out of money

again it's Monday again every day
    is Monday Barbie

Chang's mother is sleeping in the other
    room again her

father is confused by papers again
    mumbling shuffling

through them his thoughts are like
    shuffling cards that

never stop someone is bringing
    another oxygen tank

again Barbie Chang's ambitions are
    whispering again

she attaches a green heavy cylinder
    to thin tubes again

everyone at school seems rude as they
    talk about their kids

and their new skills again the women
    at school hear *illness* and

interrupt with their own stories about
    their grandmothers again

it's tense at school the Circle ignores
    her more than usual

they go to bars and do barre classes
    they go to the mall more

often while Barbie Chang mulls about
    all the people God has

killed in planes again her father refuses to
    get up from the restaurant

table because he still wants to sign the
    receipt again Anne Carson

calls metaphor a mind put in *a state of*
    *war* what if when a part

of the brain dies it can no longer be at
    war the two armies never

fight they are divided by a large hill that
    either side can never see over

what happens when a brain is frozen in
    a state of preparation

## BARBIE CHANG GOT HER HAIR DONE

Barbie Chang got her hair done for
    the school auction

she was afraid sick of the Circle since
    she heard of their

shopping for matching dresses so out
    of the nest she flew

into the auction thinking she could
    outmaneuver her

loneliness thinking she could overcome
    being classified thinking

she could be an agent of her own
    classification in came

the Circle drunk tossing coins at baskets
    one in pink one in

green one in orange one in purple
    matching floral

barrettes glowing like a rainbow that
    seemed low enough

to reach to touch Barbie Chang would
    never admit it but

she still wanted the rainbow to rain on
    her to wear bows in her

hair that meant she belonged somewhere
    else she owed it to

her children to make friends to blend
    into the dead end

## MR. DARCY TAKES BARBIE CHANG

Mr. Darcy takes Barbie Chang up
    to the planetarium

to look at stars and planets the
    more they zoom in

the more the planets look like
    houses burning

there are reasons for those domes
    those halves of things

forever separating and coming back
    together those slats in

the roof they can be controlled
    opened and closed

unlike her mouth with its red poppy its
    dark copy sometimes at

night electronic toys will go off
    thinking no one is

watching she wonders who is observing
    them two terrestrial specks

celestial sextants aligned only in the
    night if they zoom in

they will see two fingerlike test tubes
    filled with fire

## BARBIE CHANG LOVES EVITES

Barbie Chang loves Evites Paperless
    Party Posts that host her

ego patch her holes she puts barrettes
    on her heart so other

people will see her will hear her her
    heart is made of hay is

disturbingly small held in its cage she
    is never late when invited

always ready for mimesis ready to put
    on her costume to

drink mimosas her heart smells like
    moth balls jumps at

every broth bell her heart growls more
    each day she trims it with

a number 2 it's messy work missing
    her aorta by a little bit

her heart is always sort of bleeding she is
    always waiting for

invitations once she heard the Circle
    planning a birthday party

for a daughter she stationed herself
    sipped water for days

waiting for the Evite leaving her Kindle
    on as a nightlight it

glowed a blue garden on the ceiling she
    let her guard down it

never made a ringing sound when you
    brush a child's hair the

mother can also feel the pain she heard
    the ice skating party

was a hit little girls going in figure
    eights their breath

coming out in clouds shaped like
    little white hearts

These men can be collected in a cup
    or a shovel but Barbie

Chang cannot pick each out except
    by the handful they

each dress better have nice sweaters
    come with tags that say

*Do Not Remove* they move everywhere
    they are a catalogue that

keeps coming in the mail each only
    slightly different from

the last this manuscript is named
    *Man. 4* moon sounds

like man the shadow on her desk is
    not hers her light

is her heart that hurts from igniting the
    microphone she talks

into an ear but the ear is not an ear she
    can whisper into

it is her own ear she has never seen
    except backward

the words keep coming from Mr. Darcy's
    mouth and she keeps

waiting each month for him to go back
   into the book but

how does she turn her back if there is
   no one watching her

## BARBIE CHANG HAS NO INTENTION

Barbie Chang has no intention of
    letting the heart win

it's the lungs that need her shelter
    her mother's lungs

sound like Velcro they crackle like a
    candy wrapper this

year Barbie Chang has wrapped up
    the past but no matter

how many times she cuts and pastes a
    new childhood over her

old one her hair color is still algebraic
    it is both $x$ and the

solution it is metonymy for her whole
    being it is the most

economical way to identify her when
    you know someone

will die it is not economical to keep
    them alive but we try

and try because we don't know that
    good memories can't start

appearing until after someone is dead
    when waiting for someone

to die getting ahead seems foolish
    when someone is dying

there are always noises in the attic
    Barbie Chang hates the

status quo wants to go back to being
    quoted wants something

to happen cannot lie she has wished
    for someone to die

## MR. DARCY GRABS

Mr. Darcy grabs Barbie Chang's hand
   one that has a loop

and can be tugged like a leash she
   wishes his hand

were a special hand she has been trying
   to touch for years but

his hand has no breadth or texture
   fingers too big to text

just a hand that only knows one
   woman's upholstery

its fabric and stuffing Barbie Chang's
   own hand is stiff

scared of his letting go when he leaves
   her gasp comes out as an

X-ray of the other woman the
   same imposter is it

possible that she desires Mr. Darcy
   because he cannot be

captured on film because he has no
   footsteps maybe he

was right wing all along but if she
   knew that would she

give the ring back the phone rings
    every day with men

trying to sell her solar panels don't
    they know not

everything that burns should be
    captured and sold

## BARBIE CHANG'S FATHER CALLS

Barbie Chang's father calls again calls
    her again again he calls

her still knows how to dial a cellphone
    Barbie Chang's father has

another problem always has a problem
    doesn't know he is

liminal he says Barbie Chang's mother
    criticizes him all is wrong

today today he calls his hands *handles*
    today his handles hurt

today Barbie Chang's mother handles
    the bad news poorly

today the doctor thinks three months
    but says six no one can

fix Barbie Chang's mother once her
    mother had good hearing

could hear anything see and smell
    everything corners were

always too sharp too dark no hearth
    always harping on

everyone what was wrong with everyone
    too dumb too short too tall

not enough college collar too white
    moon too fraction

moon too waxing when she is not yelling
    at him or asking about the

taxes has Barbie Chang finished her
    taxes again asking about

the taxes the same taxes or whether she
    can fix his brain she lies

on her side thin body shaped
    like a large ear

## BARBIE CHANG WAITS

Barbie Chang waits for Mr. Darcy to
    reappear he is her

hound he hunts her every 43 days
    Barbie Chang has

eaten with 129 forks since then 86
    bowls of rice she still

has not achieved fame it still rains
    every day in her brain

she still falls asleep in clubs playing
    techno music

her head receives the beat her head
    is a music stand

the conductor taps it with a lightning rod
    her brain metals all

night it materials into Mr. Darcy they
    hold hands into the room

two fools who think this will last
    they will eventually

be the past too she bites his neck like
    a flea but he doesn't

swat her off there is no sweat because
    the scene is not real she

has been here before on the other twin
　　bed twining another body

but always thinking of Mr. Darcy she
　　always wakes in the same

place the same room outside could be India
　　could be a windy hallway of

a hotel room with carpet worn from
　　heavy pets at 20 she

bought $40 nail clippers full
　　of hope now she clips

twenty little fingers and twenty little
　　toes her daughter wants

to grow her hair out when it is finally
　　long she will be gone

II

## DEAR P.

1

Five seconds to open a parachute one
that smells like terror I am a river and
you a body when your body fell into
the river you informed it ignored it
I handled you as a half masted plank or
wooden vessel when I received you it was
night the constellations broke their
vertebrae arching to see you I stumbled
over myself to key you into my folds river
of error river of dirty whiteness now I know
if I press hard enough on my eyeballs I see
geometric shapes and stars my love for you
is something like this it is there like
the stars but nothing I can grab or free

2

I want to change the ending before this
begins I want to know how to begin without
the softness of sentimentality it exhales
from my pencil from the edge of my hair
through the heart as something wept seeps
down my arm through my fingers and comes
out as speech a soft speech sponge speech
a speech that speaks for me and fills this page
with seaweed green swaths of love I cross them
out force new words storm words out through
a straw but they take the shape of a girl's
handwriting there's a heart on the lowercase *i*
it looks like a microphone and when I sing into
it my voice comes back softer like a lullaby

3

There you are on your back sleeping
looking dead I now dread the long day
filled with people I no longer care for I am
your pupil now you tell me what to study
here there are no rejections no Mello Roos
no asters with their clusters of flowers
hiding weeds no new poets taking selfies
or being blessed they fade more each day
out of your pupil I see a room as large
as a ruby and that is your world the whole
of it how I love what you see the part the
particle of a partitioned place one yet in
need of reform a world where others' words
can yet burn into you like a branding iron


4

The scientific has gone what's left are fires
that can't be packaged that whisk my love
into threads I cannot collect or control
frequencies here have no waveform just
dotted lines everything has excavated
itself and everything has altered in the way
water in a pool breaks up light into pieces in
the way the light is tranced into approximations
and deviations into eyeless swirls that never
fix I have borne witness to this giant this
love for you that never leaves that burrows
laterally and downward that layers and
imprints on my skin the way goggles leave a
mark long after I have taken them off

## 5

When you wake your feet will be longer
you will be interested in the moles and
the dark holes in the pumpkin's face
you will point and laugh at the citrus
comedy of its body you will scream when
I take a rake away stamp your heels as if
removing snow *no no no no* I am afraid of
your moods your streaks I cannot stack or
break I am afraid of the next minute the
atomic equivalent of death the endless
present tense I approach you as I do a
cigarette butt at the park I am suspicious of
you handle you by the burnt out bits the
side untouched by your sucking lips

## 6

Suddenly your face resembles mine but
how fast the look is swallowed into the
celestial space and your face is yours again
how terribly I want to inhabit your face
to dive into its cells to fold into your
gossamer skin how terribly I want to be the
side upon which you depend the part that
is only used to hold you up if you'd kiss me
you'd know the slum of my skin twisted with
weeds and wilderness old skin that has tried
to fly but cannot fly look there it is again
a look I know how quickly it tangents like
a small fish into a rock there are dangers
in the sea there is sincerity in the sea

7

When you fall onto the floor your cry
sounds like a lightbulb as it pulses on
off on off your wail sticks to me I fail to
hear the people dying or the dog crying or
the seizures that light up bodies you are my
seizure a blowtorch that spouts fire then
laughter then fire you take me by force you
are a sudden occurrence I ask the sky for
help but it just gives me the next rain I ask
the rain for help it just gives me the square
root of rain which is just more rain I ask
the fig tree for help but it just gives me little
brown pamphlets when I ask the tree which
way it just points in every direction


8

Someone says it is difficult to write poems
that are both domestic and ambitious if your
small head is my earth if I have concerns only
for the internal affairs of your body then how
am I domestic our home has more than four
sides there are wars in rooms furniture in
formation if I am your domestic servant why is
it assumed we are domestic that we are small
and petty that we are controllable unwild you
betray me over and over I play you and prey
on you this is not domestic there is no floral
sofa no salad plate no bingo hall just falling
bodies the trouble with falling bodies is
someone needs to catch them

9

I must tell you something there were six
lights in a circle a large wreath of heat that
tried to drag open my eyes I woke up coughing
but the lights were missing it was sudden
there was no heartbeat an extra chromosome
my boy let the suction take it turn its body
into a latticework of tissue lying on the table
I remembered the man helping his boy with
cerebral palsy walk the boy's legs bent stiff as
if climbing a ladder to God there must be a
God only God makes me listen this way I take
my quill and write God a note but there are no
more words they have flown beyond the lights
all the letters shaped like question marks

10

You are no longer fictional no longer the
other side of a cliff you are my phantom
limb you glean even when gone you are
a sensation an illusion a missing you are
earthbound titanic you make me itch and
burn and ache when you touch the flower's
thorn my own hand explodes when your
head goes underwater my sight is taken by
white only when I am alone underwater the
light streaming into the pool like bars my ears
filled with the water's prayer are you gone
I slump into a temperate zone but then it rains
your thoughts are all around me and they
dimple the water like desire

11

When a boy throws sand on your face
the hunter's bow and arrow tucked behind
my choking heart bends and I must do
everything to suppress otherwise to summon
the wren in me the festival but how lovely
his round face would look pocked with
sand how happy my hand would be to throw
grains toward his face into the plumbing
of a body I care little about here a giant ficus
tree can lift up a sidewalk here I am lean with
only a canister of water I am broken down in
this valley no goodwill I am embroidered
with love and grief with the exact moment
your breathing becomes slow and deep


12

The sun sends its wires of heat onto your
face stops on your cheek coiling into a
present tense of red I am a hungry bird
that murmurs love that murmurs more
when I see red it is not blood or war it is
not the spur on the point of fishhooks
the red here is a tributary toward you it is
a ruby of lunar rules a stone of sixty
sides I want to ladle your ruddy rust taste
your cheek that feels like church against
my lips your terrestrial material the softest
my mouth has found your skin that dies
each year your sheen that blights that
forever barriers me from you

13

Your thoughts come out as frays as howls
they are like the bubbles from a fish's mouth
that rise and disappear globules of letters in
a liquid envelope today a woman's voice
sounds old wood thick deep the voice is
mine it takes deeper cover against the sky
against its blue shin that never answers with
anything but clouds and rain my voice digs
with its fingers in the wrong direction dead
down it goes head down my throat drags me
one day I will bang and bang on the soil from
below but you and your briefcase will not hear
me one day you will look down at the manhole
pass through my breath rising up as steam


14

A bench sits stares out to sea it says *sit
and feel this here* another looks at the swamp
onto the logarithmic sways of thistle I close
my eyes and still see you I plug my ears
and still hear you let us pass the bench
and its lathed feelings let me bite the sky
away from the seam of ocean let me grieve
you and play you irk you and deter you let
me be happy with the *of* of love the square
root of you let me stop wanting the whole
let us stand on earth and watch ourselves
play toss with the yellow ball from where we
are from eye level not through a photograph
not a video not from space not later

15

In poetry accident is in vogue the idea of
wandering into a forest and running into a
flock of owls who normally work alone I
used to hunt for the owl and its highbrow
nose spellbound by its *oooo oooo* but we
planned you induced you told you when
now the sunlight plans your naps we eat not
when rain strikes our magnolia but when the
sun angles onto the axis of your back how
much accident even in planning you have
become my broken English how in one
moment your hands collide as in clapping
how in some other moment they will rise
over my encased body touch in prayer

III

## THE DOCTOR SAYS HOSPICE

The doctor says hospice as if she
    is a hostess and

wants Barbie Chang to try the
    crawfish there are

no longer many crawl spaces left for
    her mother who no

longer can take her own showers
    once she cut flowers

but now her lungs are burnt crust
    lost in their own

rusting Barbie Chang always thought
    her mother was heartless

not lungless but now she knows the
    lungs were framed

a pair of slabs tricked by the heart
    traitors to each other

even the lungs want to socially identify
    with others to climb

higher search for something better
    climbing up a ladder into

the sky is another way of drowning
    their punishment is

scars that grow into honeycombs
    there's nothing scarier

than something that won't stop fooling
    you with its beauty

## MR. DARCY COMES AGAIN

Mr. Darcy comes again through
    the uneven grass in

a blue cape boots long hair a white
    shirt with sleeves that

cover his palms the terminal part of
    his body but nothing

terminal here even silence is not
    silent Barbie Chang

sits again at terminal E gate 33 and
    waits for a plane that

never arrives there are eyes on the
    runways in the fog

planes look like nightgowns the people
    in the airport don't

speak they only gasp her gasp when
    she sees the man again

in the fog in the threads of the trees
    she wants to be the girl

who wrestles a man's heart into a
    balcony into something

more than four parts she wants to
    wrestle the same man's

heart over and over but what if there
    are at least nine hearts

what if she only has one balcony is this
    why her gasp is trapped

in her throat she wants the gasp to
    elope in the form of

something other than a man she wants
    to throw up the gasp so

she can finally be free of its ring and
    creep she wants it to

leave her alone wants it to leave
    wants it

## BARBIE CHANG VOWS TO QUIT

Barbie Chang vows to quit watching
    the Circle as they go to

lunch lifted up in their own wind winding
    through the parking lot in

hot plumes she vows to quit watching
    their children in pools

together on plastic animals she tells
    herself she is more

than a gesture has some stature is ready
    to work for space her

muscles ache as she collegiates her
    children so in the

future they paint pictures of themselves
    with black hair become

more than someone else's grieving
    because everyone has

debt with the sun because at night things
    become clear again windows

light up like presents in one a boy with
    cerebral palsy in a ball

laughing his body stiff in the shape of an
    empty lawn chair

## BARBIE CHANG'S TEARS

Barbie Chang's tears are the lights of
    the city that go off on

off on Mr. Darcy walks around the city
    but Barbie Chang can't

follow him she can't promote herself
    if she had legs she would

stop begging if she had hands she would
    stop her own wedding

the city has no extra bedding it is not
    ready yet the maids are

still making beds Barbie Chang is still
    looking for small openings

there are always storms long arms drinks
    with pink umbrellas

because they know she is confused like a
    sea horse light avoids her

town on the map B2 C4 she wants to
    be used she doesn't

want to be with you or you it is morning
    again and she is already

mourning the men the night men who
    never fight who never

write back she prefers to sleep on her
    back so she can see the

eyes of her attackers in the morning
    a bed with questions

with her depression on each side two
    small holes from knees

## THERE ARE LUNGS

There are lungs in Barbie Chang's
    dreams and jeeps in her

lungs the lungs are hard and almost
    dead the jeep no longer

runs her mother's lungs are undone
    they cover her heart like

a tarp her mother thinks her own
    heart is softer than it is

Barbie Chang thought her own heart
    would do more than

beat she longs for a longer lawn where
    she can sit on a mower

and not think about perimeters if a
    heart doesn't beckon

forever why does it matter if we ever
    reach language why does

it matter which form is better or whether
    anyone ever wins an

award for anything maybe her life is
    scarce because it's not

about filling up but emptying out like
    the tree the men trim

every four years how it just grows
    another way creeping

under the driveway Barbie Chang is still
    working harder because

the women at school seem better and
    healthier have better

breath and time and rhyme with each
    other when they speak

some of them pretend to be wealthy
    if they pretend then

why does she want a new house bigger
    than theirs frost still

covers her old windows winter still
    comes with its lows

even the snow is the same color each
    year never worse never

better sometimes powder sometimes
    wetter sometimes earlier

but always still in power no elections
    to topple the leaders snow

does not fall it is thrown down at the
    people for protesting used

to punish the people by making us
    dig ourselves out

## MR. DARCY GROWS

Mr. Darcy grows in Barbie Chang
    like a deficit she

requires a radioactive suit three
    thousand thistles

come down thoughts of him attack
    her like a shower

once Sylvia ran outside to chase a boy
    who didn't stop to

visit her all the faces in the street
    looked rigid except

for his what if we throw a rope up to
    Heaven and nothing

pulls back we are always on one side
    or the other a balloon

is waiting to be shaped into a dog or
    it has just fallen out

of shape there's always a vibrating
    diving board that

means we can't tell if he is coming
    or has just left

## BARBIE CHANG'S DAUGHTER

Barbie Chang's daughter befriends the
   new girl at school but

before they can form a bond the new girl's
   mom tells Barbie Chang

that her own daughter should not tie
   herself down too fast and

in one week the new girl walks past
   Barbie Chang's daughter

no longer talks to her the mother works
   hard to send cards to

the Circle one by one she stars their names
   because they are free

to star names free to have stars next to
   their names Barbie Chang

can no longer play dead because she
   must be seen to play dead

she realizes she is not what others name
   her would we name a

deer something else if it could see the
   ocean would the deer

even name itself a deer if we've never
   seen a deer does it mean

it doesn't exist if Barbie Chang perches
    on a hill with binoculars

waiting for deer and sees someone else
    looking for deer but

watching her instead does that mean she
    exists or that she's a deer

## THEN BARBIE CHANG

Then Barbie Chang and Mr. Darcy
    are in the backseat

of a car kissing not the light kind
    but one where their

hands are on each other's cheeks
    holding each other's

heads as if they will fall off why does
    so much love come at

the beginning then disappear then
    once again at the

moment before death why can't the
    same kind exist in

between in the breaths in the afternoon
    in the sitting room

little girls dress like princesses one pink
    one blue one yellow they

wear plastic heels because they still think
    they will never fall

## BARBIE CHANG KEEPS WATCHING

Barbie Chang keeps watching
    the Ellen Pao trial

wants her to win thinks she is right
    thinks she should fight

thinks she is wrong thinks she should
    step down Barbie Chang

remembers her own long days in a
    cubicle with Rob Meyer

mitering his edges talking about his
    dates with Asian women

the ones who made it like Eileen never
    complained smart ones

didn't want to work at Walmart switched
    off the office lights each

night Barbie Chang like Ellen Pao kept
    good records never wore

corduroys to work pretended she hated
    recreation with other

Asians she can't help but think that
    Ellen Pao is not pretty

is petty is not good to powwow with
    probably doesn't own

UGG boots if Barbie Chang were her boss
    she might have also booted

her out of the office full of lies because
    of her small fisted eyes

## BARBIE CHANG WANTS TO BE SOMEONE

Barbie Chang wants to be someone
    special to no longer

have wet hair to no longer be spectral
    to be a spectacle Barbie

Chang wants to befriend the Academy
    which is the Circle

wants to eat meat with the Academy
    wants to share with the

cads who think there is a door to the
    Academy wants the key to

the Academy door wants to give grants
    and awards for words

but she never knew that life was about
    unraveling not raveling

that a tear is only a tear after it has
    fallen her parents never

called in favors never knew there was an
    Academy never learned

alchemy Barbie Chang wants to forgive
    the Academy for its

cattiness wants to hate the Academy
    and its Circle and their

certainty each year she buys climbing
        shoes to go up the tree

she tries but can't climb then sells them
        on Craigslist she gets a

new pair each year on her wish list but
        can't get past the first five

feet she stays on the street rolls herself
        flat so she can become

the street feel the bare feet of people
        pressing her deeper into

the earth there are aspirations of worth
        everywhere a stipple of

ants around the cement crack frozen
        from bug spray as if

they had meant to take the shape
        of an iris

## IN THE END ELIZABETH

In the end Elizabeth just wanted the
    house and a horse not

much more what if Mr. Darcy didn't
    own the house or

worse not even a horse how do we
    separate the things

from a man the man from the things
    is a man still the same

without his reins here it rains every
    fifteen minutes it

would be foolish to marry a man
    without an umbrella

did Cinderella really love the prince or
    just the prints on the

curtains in the ballroom once Barbie
    Chang went window

shopping but didn't want a window
    when do you know it's

time to get a new man one who can win
    more things at the fair

Barbie Chang already has four stuffed
    pandas from the fair she

won fair and square is it time to be less
　　square to wear something

more revealing in *North and South* she
　　does the dealing gives him

the money but she falls in love with him
　　when he has the money

when he is still ruling if the water is
　　running in the other

room is it wrong for her to not want
　　to chase it because she

wants to taste it when she waves to
　　a man she loves what

happens when another man with a lot
　　more bags waves back

## IS IT RUDE FOR BARBIE CHANG

Is it rude for Barbie Chang to tell men
    she doesn't love them

just the idea of them what if we don't
    even love living but just

the idea of it pictures always look
    lovely but it was an

ugly day if women were actually paid
    the same as men would

we all just pass on the highest bidder
    who says it's a privilege

to be romantic romance with its antics
    and its time limits like the

nut that never tells us or other nuts
    when it will let go

we stand under the tree ready to
    collect them with our

arms wide open as in waltzing who
    authored the word *love*

does anyone know the author's original
    intent does it matter

that no one knows exactly what it means
    does it matter that it

might signify everything what if we never
    needed a word for it

what if it is shapeless and composed
    of gestures if we name

the thing *love* it doesn't mean it
    will last a nut does its

best to last but at some point just falls
    like all the others before it

## BARBIE CHANG'S MOTHER CALLS

Barbie Chang's mother calls her to
    tell her about the

oxygen machine that outfoxes her
    father he can't figure

out how to turn it on there's a whole
    generation of people

who care about deer porn not form her
    dog only cares about the

deer horn she gave him yesterday Barbie
    Chang's father who bothers

with everyone's business doesn't know
    what Bisquick is someone

wrote a book of poems about Kanye
    West there are still

old poets looking for the best new young
    poets who are all hornets

around the same old nest Barbie Chang
    knows she lives in an

America that most people don't care
    about on most days

she can't distinguish between being a
    token and racism she

either feels like a token or is experiencing
    racism a token needs to be

acted upon by a subject but the same is
    true of racism does that

mean her whole life is an object as a
    shadow of someone

else on some days she has feeling in
    her lungs tries her

mother's oxygen machine the $O_2$ owes
    her nothing it goes

through her body breathing for a
    shadow is just a hobby

## ONCE A MAN SAID EVERYTHING

Once a man said everything Barbie
    Chang wanted to hear

except she is deaf sometimes she
    wonders about the

depth of her love for others or is she
    simply diving to eat

better although she is deaf she hears
    there are oysters at the

bottom she can't get them because
    once she has applied

sunscreen on her children her hands
    are greasy her palms

are pale from trying to wipe out desire
    what if everything on

the bottom is really rotten and our ends
    are already written

what if there are no verbs just nouns
    what if saying something

makes it true what if becoming a
    witness instead of a

victim were as simple as words a wrist
    can't hold much

weight the man hanging out of the tower
    was forced out by the

smoke or made a choice to exit the
    window he held on to

a rope until his hands slipped if he could
    orient himself headfirst

we could say he wasn't falling but
    actually diving

## BARBIE CHANG REFUSES

Barbie Chang refuses to start her
    own Circle refuses

to wear a girdle would she think
    about the Circle in

the last eight minutes before the
    plane crashed into

the mountains there are thousands
    of miles between the

land and the sky between the words
    *to love* and *loved* there are

little boats in the brain that can row
    nowhere Barbie Chang

should not mind about all her kind
    whether she is pretty or

skinny enough loved enough once in
    Yosemite she stared for

hours at two giant sequoias fused
    together at the base but

separate high above the plaque said they
    *must be in love* she knew it

wasn't true that they were really two
    trees trying to leave

## IN AND OUT THESE MEN GO

In and out these men go in Barbie
    Chang's life and run

her life too many run ins and starings
    how do they see her

lies so clearly then they disappear it
    might be months before

she sees them again once she saw one
    every day from afar

but then he moved now she is only
    moved by movies the

in and out the losing under the frozen
    river there are still things

moving when did her footprints stack up
    like a deck of cards

when did having change to dying
    the mother in a child's

drawing is always smiling but why are
    her eyes always

two large holes if you must have an
    answer ask the

body it is the only thing that aspires
    toward failure

## SOME DAYS BARBIE CHANG

Some days Barbie Chang wants to
 hang up her Asian boots

and root for the Circle she wakes up
 not proud to be what

she is in a sea of water who gets to
 decide which section

of water eats the ship it's always the
 white water that

devours first there are towers of people
 working in America

people all aiming for emeritus she can't
 figure out how to open

the door of the tower someone keeps
 lowering her down to

the roof but doesn't give her a rule book
 her mother gave her the

wrong rouge a ruler with no lines still
 Barbie Chang doesn't

want to appear rude so she waits on the
 roof of Paul Muldoon's

building she wonders if she is standing on
 Paul Muldoon's head how

she wishes to win the Guggenheim like
    Paul Muldoon to doom

others like Paul Muldoon to write
    rejection letters sending

them out the *New Yorker* windows
    sometimes in the winter

the letters take the snow down like
    dumbwaiters

## BARBIE CHANG SHOULD HAVE SEEN

Barbie Chang should have seen
    the signs should

have noticed the signs in the street
    that were backward

that were in a different language
    should have noticed

the people hiding behind trees in front
    of her mother's house

her mother catching her breath after
    a shower little pieces

of death rubbed off by the towel
    for two years her car

never moved then her body hardly
    moved death is

fragmented is not a noun but a series
    of verbs its movements

nearly invisible Barbie Chang visited each
    day with her wagon of

food guns ready to shoot the dragons
    under the bed to shoot

the dementia out of her father's head
    she should have seen

the signs but was busy tending to her
    children busy sleeping with

both eyes closed she was tired of her
    mother tired of her

anger toward her father tired of her
    father's stunned weather

his errors tired of their errands tired
    of her lungs and their

refusal to open the hospice notebook
    said *7:14 can't breathe*

then *7:34 last breath* the word *death* hiding
    in the word *breath* all

along she never saw her take her
    second to last breath

never saw her wait twenty seconds wait
    for Barbie Chang to come

see her wait for Barbie Chang to punch
    holes in her lungs

Barbie Chang couldn't find the hole puncher
    wanted to punch herself for

not singing to her for not medicating
    her father for not

believing her mother about her father for
    not combining the word

*death* with an object for thinking death has
  a shape is something

containable like a cup of water for thinking
  death has no sound even

snow falls in syllables why do we kill
  flowers for a funeral when

there is already so much death fifty people
  came to the wake where

were all the people before where was
  Barbie Chang when she

took one more breath when she blew
  out her last wrath

## BARBIE CHANG IS DONE

Barbie Chang is done worshipping the
    Circle is done shopping

for a matching purple dress she is
    complete with three

plates and doesn't need more she now
    knows there is darkness

behind darkness she decides to form
    her own Circle not to

irk the Circle but to create something
    new to build a new system

out of sticks a new road out of clay
    instead of complain

planes keep falling from the sky even
    the planes need someone

to give them direction to point them down
    the bodies are in little

pieces on the ground the little pieces
    have no more relation to

each other no one is weeping because
    of the smells she bends

down and picks up small pieces of
    people puzzle sized

pieces tries to put the different colors
    together a million piece

puzzle of the world's troubles that she
    must leave on the

table for her daughters to put back
    together outside a box

of staples loose on the driveway even the
    earth is coming undone

## BARBIE CHANG POKES THROUGH

Barbie Chang pokes through her
    mother's purse

the little brown hearse of lipstick and
    blush her mother would

have let her go through her purse
    because she pursued

her mother's dreams her mother's last
    call on her last cellphone

on June 19 what was Barbie Chang
    doing on June 19 she

was thinking about the moon she hasn't
    looked at for 91 months

and how the moon was a medal she
    wanted around her neck

she was probably thinking about the
    Circle of women at

school or circling and striking words
    shifting points of view

thinking about how an acorn with its
    small hat to cover it is

a metaphor for truth now she is left with
    small images of her

mother that come and hover and leave
    whenever they please

little hummingbirds of death such as how
    her mother wanted

a Sprite but couldn't remember the name
    for it how her eyes looked

slightly crossed the day before she died
    how she could only

breathe through her abdomen that
    went up and down

like the machine the body isn't how
    her stillness was

deafening how she was warm for
    so long after

# HOW ALONE BARBIE CHANG'S MOTHER

How alone Barbie Chang's mother
    must have felt doing

nothing but dying her mother actually
    stopped dyeing her hair

in January stopped being an actuary
    for her money she

must have known her time was limited
    did the diseased birch

tree know they were going to cut it down
    how quickly the air

around it filled in the space it does no
    good to know a mother's

face who would have known that a
    mother's face could

be erased too at some point we are all
    eliminated from this

earth at some point most of us give birth
    at some point we lose

a mother at some point we are all
    disappointments who

can't possibly care for others when
    our mothers die we

are all lost and there are no words for
    it some want to

name us as grieving others wrongly
    name us heroes

## DEAR P.

There   will be   a circle   of girls there will  be

many circles of      girls   who turn into circles of

women   there will be many    parties many grills with

corn and   meat losing its red center   there will

also be   a circle of crows who circle the     circle of

boars   who circle      the circle of grass     work

their way   into its center there will be a     circle

of gnats   who   circle the dirty      boars because

there   are      awards for   grouping   easier  than

absence   easier than working against    easier than

separating   water   with curtains   good things are

often in   pieces   are backing        away     from

doorways   are alone   the heart is    alone  in

our   bodies   because      it must be   to   love

## DEAR P.

Let her    let them collect others    let them hurl depth

over the balcony  in the    meantime    it's not about

purpose but about the    person    buy stackables and

store    your  selves in them    let    everyone in though

don't pull the curtains closed or snap the buttons shut

the girls might try to    come in    might try to throw

you out    woe you    the boys might    lure you    out

please don't    kowtow    to them        the wars aren't

real there are    three ways    to    still        everyone

with love    don't eat the    meat of your    enemies

because it tastes just like    your tongue    don't meet

them in the        middle just    jump in the    puddle

together    and    fill in the    white    space    the wind is

fine    with being    homeless but we are    not    the wind

## DEAR P.

Someone will     love you   many will      love

you      many will brother you   some of these

loves will     bother you   some   will     leave you

one might     haunt   you     hunt you in your

sleep     make you      weep the tearless kind of

weep the      kind of weep   that drowns your

organs   slowly   there are little oars  in your body

little boats   grab on to them and row and      row

someone will tell you     *no*     but you won't   know

he is   right until you have     already      wrung your

own heart dry   your hands dripping knives    until

you have    already   reached your hands into     his

body and put them through his     heart     love is

the only thing that     is not   an     argument

## DEAR P.

If you are    like me and can    only see the horizon

that is unreachable   don't know that want   sheds and

grows and      sheds and      grows    please don't

keep trying              the outline   is fine find a closer

aisle  pull the cans and boxes      from the shelves   so

you can   eat    so you can feed on likeness    anything

is possible but   the possible isn't always      foldable

it's okay to not spin the    diamond   that begs for your

finger  it's okay to   reach   behind you   allow your clothes

to   snag onto   air   to hide in   time    to exist in

the stars  to believe that awards   signify   nothing  it is

okay to only watch the birds in the   ficus tree clutter  the

branches each season   leave    their waste   and let

your hands be    hands    and the   wings be   wings

## DEAR P.

Please    forage   please do not   achieve please

stay    mischievous even   if    others are deviously

perfect   your previous hair color will always be   black

black isn't    absence    black shouldn't be  auctioned

black   has options even if you have to    hack something

rip something    lengthwise    your soul   isn't a

flagpole   it can   lift up    into the sky and   wave

become    frayed    you too can   have    but make

sure   you actually   want otherwise   stay    home

and make your own   wontons   they won't    get

stuck to your tonsils    someday   someone will seal you

out    but someday someone will also   sing to   you

from a    windowsill and   steal   you    from me

because you were   never    only mine

## DEAR P.

One night   the power    in your house     will

disappear    apparitions    will appear    your

appetite will     disappear you will be left    with

only     dark and gray ghosts who      know you

more than     anyone   do not    light a candle or find

a     flashlight do not try    to    shape the pain    do

not find any    lights that     cut darkness    into  pieces

let night pile   up  there is peace     in    darkness there are

no    loudspeakers in    darkness    all tears are    equal    in

darkness    underneath    the coat      of   blinding    night

is    truth     and the difference    between truth      and

everything   else is  that     you can see     everything else

don't worry    everything you     reluctantly     give me

you will     eventually get    back

## DEAR P.

Now that my heart is    nailed onto the wall    an open

pumping splashing republic I can    imagine its last leaden

beat    I can see your arms reaching      for its slab  as

it drains    until only a gray eyed god    glares down on you

listen    the world will stand up    will    crawl    will      hire

you will    ignore you    when you grow unpin the heart    rinse

it    put it in a jar by the light    punch  holes in the lid  walk

outside      the wind will try    to welt you wilt you      weld

you      do      not let it italicize you      make you    write

complete    sentences    turn around      open        your

mouth the wind will    fill you up with      my      words

until you    stretch until      you wrest until you    recognize

yourself    until you      see that      every      woman

begins      and    ends      with      another      woman

## ACKNOWLEDGMENTS

Thank you to the editors of the journals in which many of the poems in this book appeared, often in earlier forms:

Academy of American Poets Poem-a-Day, *AGNI*, *The American Poetry Review*, *At Length*, *Blackbird*, *Chaparral*, *Diode*, *Fourteen Hills*, *Harvard Review*, *Mānoa*, *Meridian*, *Michigan Quarterly Review*, *Mississippi Review*, *Narrative*, *New England Review*, *New Republic*, *Poetry*, *Poetry International*, *Salt Hill*, *Southwest Review*, *Virginia Quarterly Review*, and *Waxwing*.

Thanks to all my friends and supporters, particularly Ilya Kaminsky for our marathon manuscript exchanges and chats about poetry.

Thanks to my comrades G.C. Waldrep, Dana Levin, and John Gallaher for the continual conversation and for always challenging my thinking. Thanks to C. Dale Young for the long-term advice and constant good humor. Thanks to all my other friends and supporters whom I confide in and rely on — too many to mention here.

Thanks to Michael Wiegers and Copper Canyon Press for everything you do for poetry.

Thanks to the Guggenheim Foundation for a fellowship and support.

And thanks to my family for tolerating my sometimes intolerable obsession with reading and writing.

Victoria Chang's previous collections of poetry are *The Boss, Salvinia Molesta,* and *Circle. The Boss* won the PEN Center USA Literary Award and a California Book Award. In 2017, she received a Guggenheim Foundation Fellowship. Her children's picture book, *Is Mommy?,* illustrated by Marla Frazee, was a New York Times Notable Book. She holds degrees from the University of Michigan, Harvard, and Stanford, as well as an MFA from Warren Wilson, where she received a Holden Scholarship. She lives in Southern California with her family and two wiener dogs, Mustard and Ketchup. She currently teaches creative writing at Chapman University and the Orange County School of the Arts. You can find her at www.victoriachangpoet.com.

Poetry is vital to language and living. Since 1972, Copper Canyon Press has published extraordinary poetry from around the world to engage the imaginations and intellects of readers, writers, booksellers, librarians, teachers, students, and donors.

## WE ARE GRATEFUL FOR THE MAJOR SUPPORT PROVIDED BY:

THE PAUL G. ALLEN
FAMILY FOUNDATION

CULTURE

Anonymous

Jill Baker and Jeffrey Bishop

Donna and Matt Bellew

John Branch

Diana Broze

Sarah and Tim Cavanaugh

Janet and Les Cox

Mimi Gardner Gates

Linda Gerrard and Walter Parsons

Gull Industries, Inc.
on behalf of Ruth and William True

The Trust of Warren A. Gummow

Steven Myron Holl

Phil Kovacevich and Eric Wechsler

Lakeside Industries, Inc.
on behalf of Jeanne Marie Lee

TO LEARN MORE ABOUT UNDERWRITING
COPPER CANYON PRESS TITLES,
PLEASE CALL 360-385-4925 EXT. 103

WE ARE GRATEFUL FOR THE MAJOR SUPPORT PROVIDED BY:

National
Endowment
for the Arts
arts.gov

ART WORKS.

OFFICE OF ARTS & CULTURE

SEATTLE

Maureen Lee and Mark Busto
Rhoady Lee and Alan Gartenhaus
Ellie Mathews and Carl Youngmann as The North Press
Anne O'Donnell and John Phillips
Petunia Charitable Fund and advisor Elizabeth Hebert
Suzie Rapp and Mark Hamilton
Joseph C. Roberts
Jill and Bill Ruckelshaus
Cynthia Lovelace Sears and Frank Buxton
Kim and Jeff Seely
Catherine Eaton Skinner and David Skinner
Dan Waggoner
Austin Walters
Barbara and Charles Wright
The dedicated interns and faithful volunteers
of Copper Canyon Press

The Chinese character for poetry is made up of two parts: "word" and "temple." It also serves as pressmark for Copper Canyon Press.

This book is set in Scala, designed for digital composition by Martin Majoor. Titles are set in Sackers Gothic based on type for engraved stationery and social cards by Gary Sackers. Book interior design by VJB/Scribe. Printed on archival-quality paper.